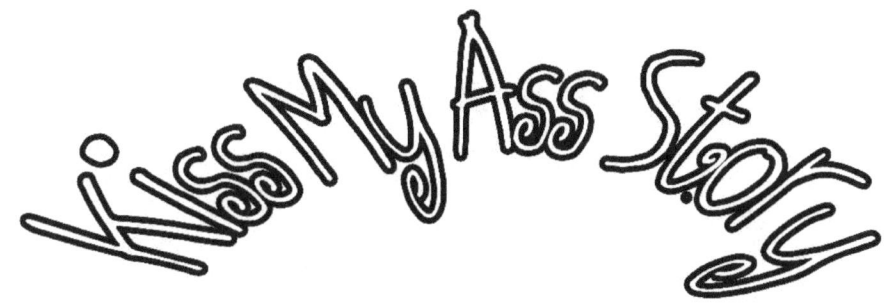

# Kiss My Ass Story

## Adorable Swear Word To Color

## FOR STRESS RELEASING

### By

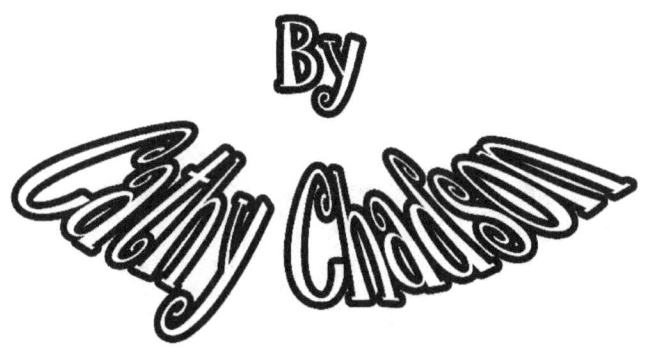

Cathy Chadison

*Happy Coloring*

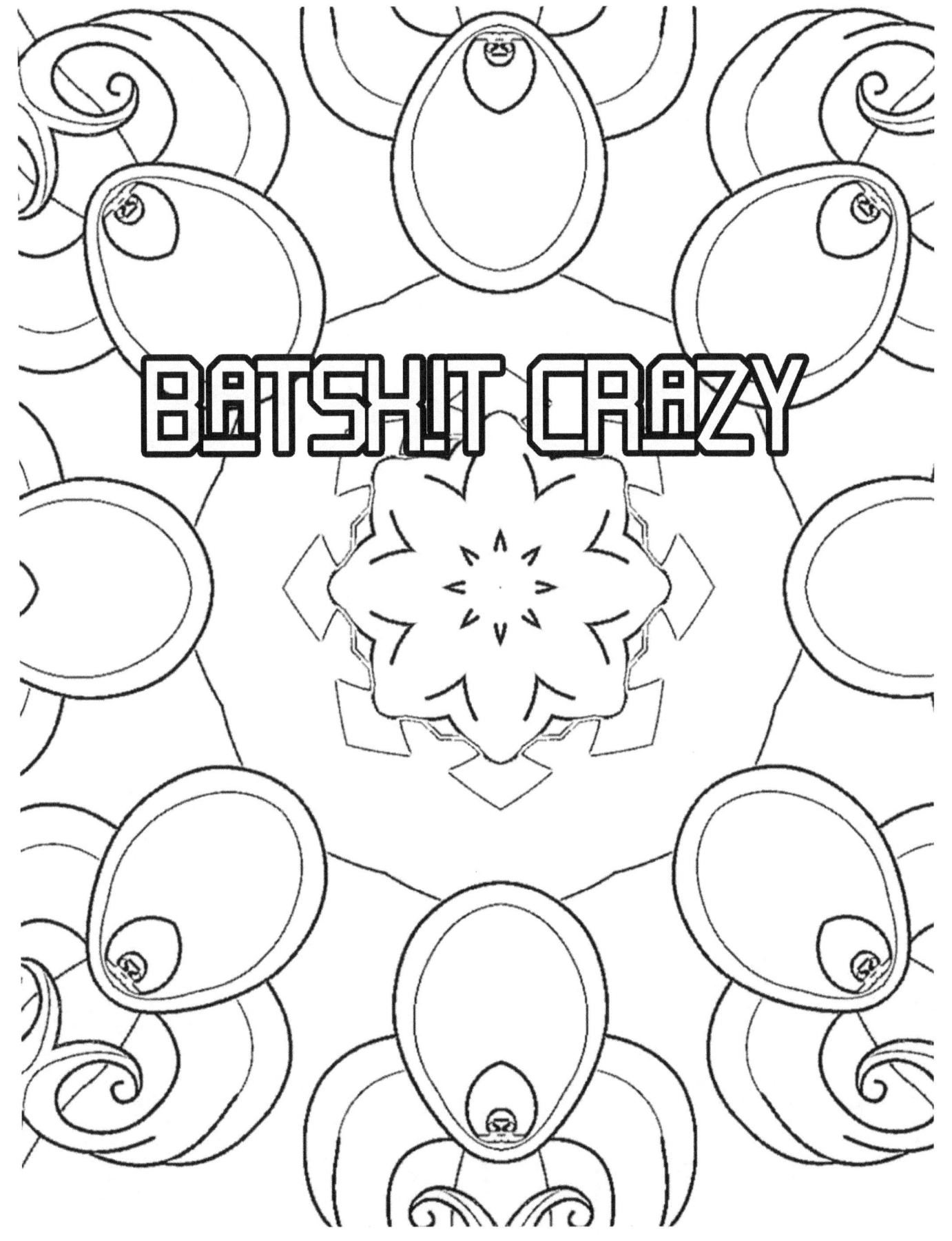

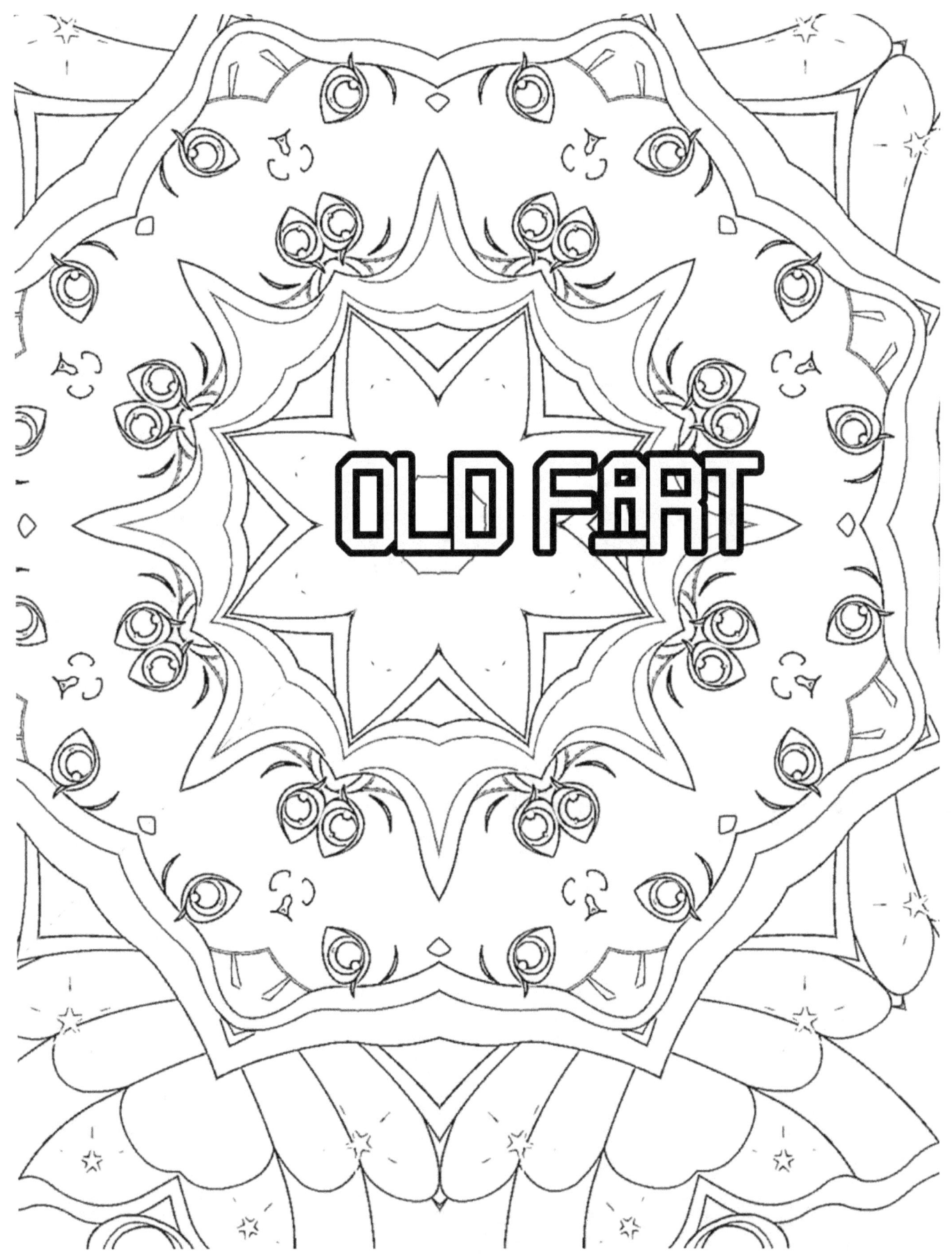

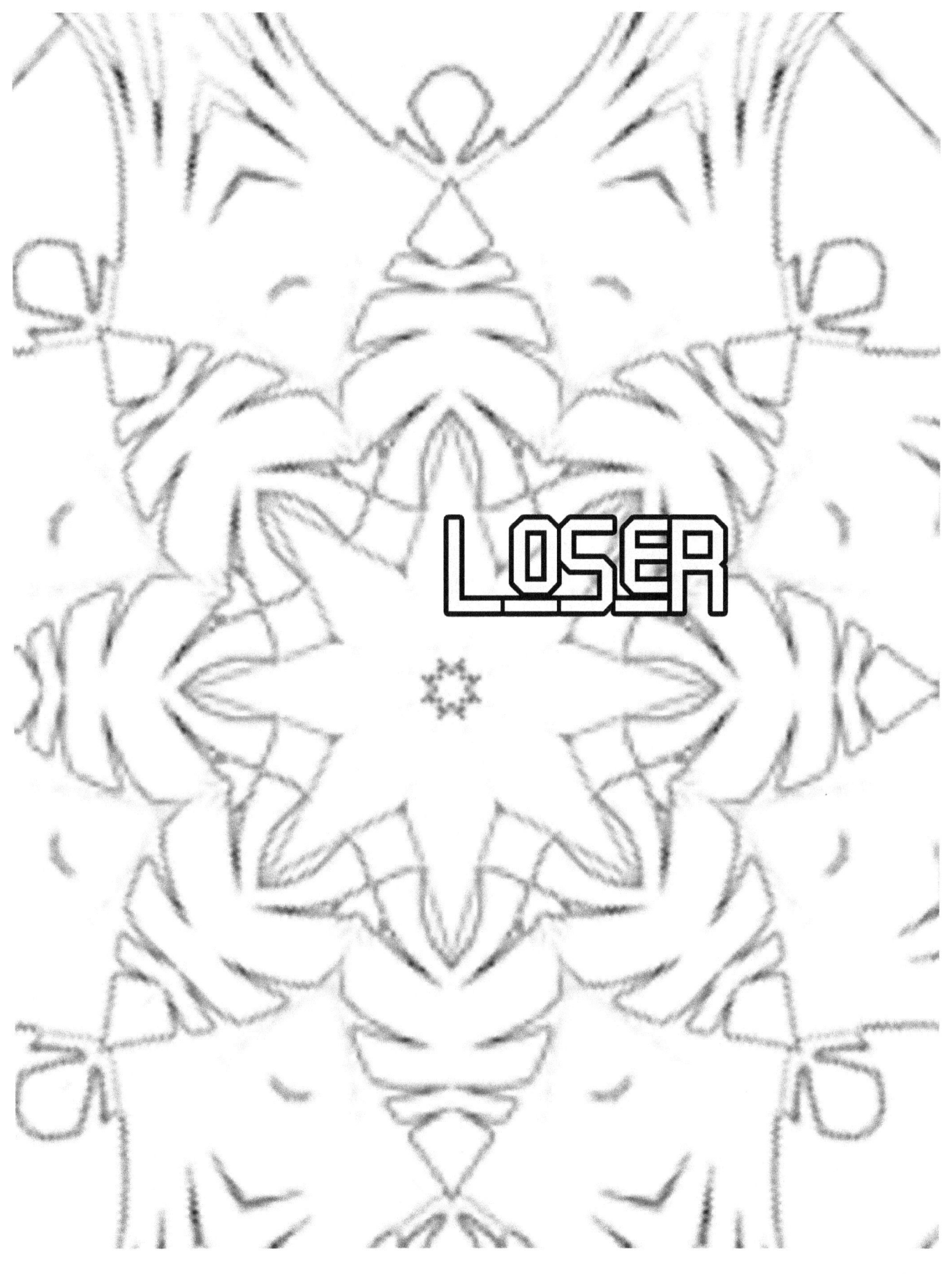

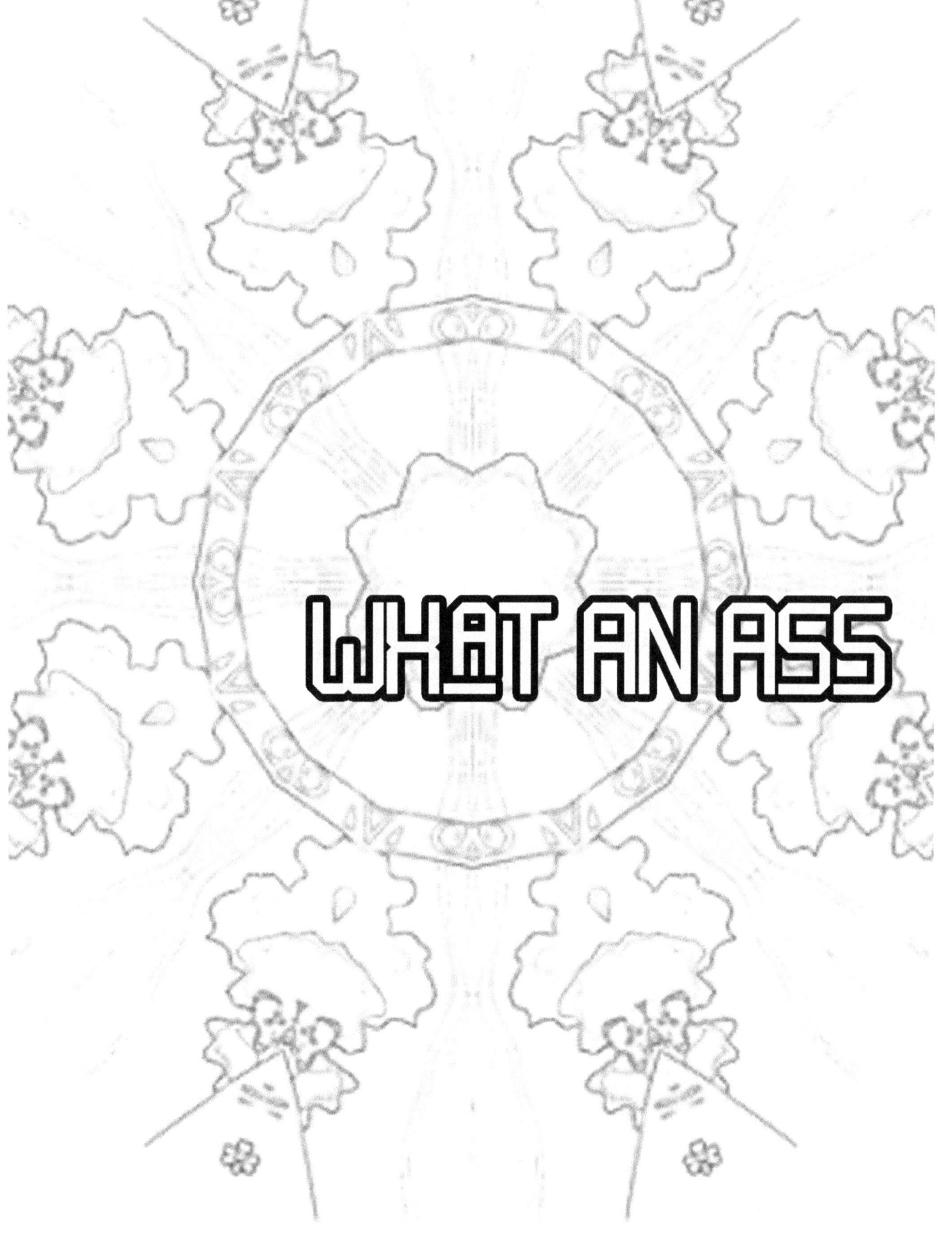

CUNT FACE

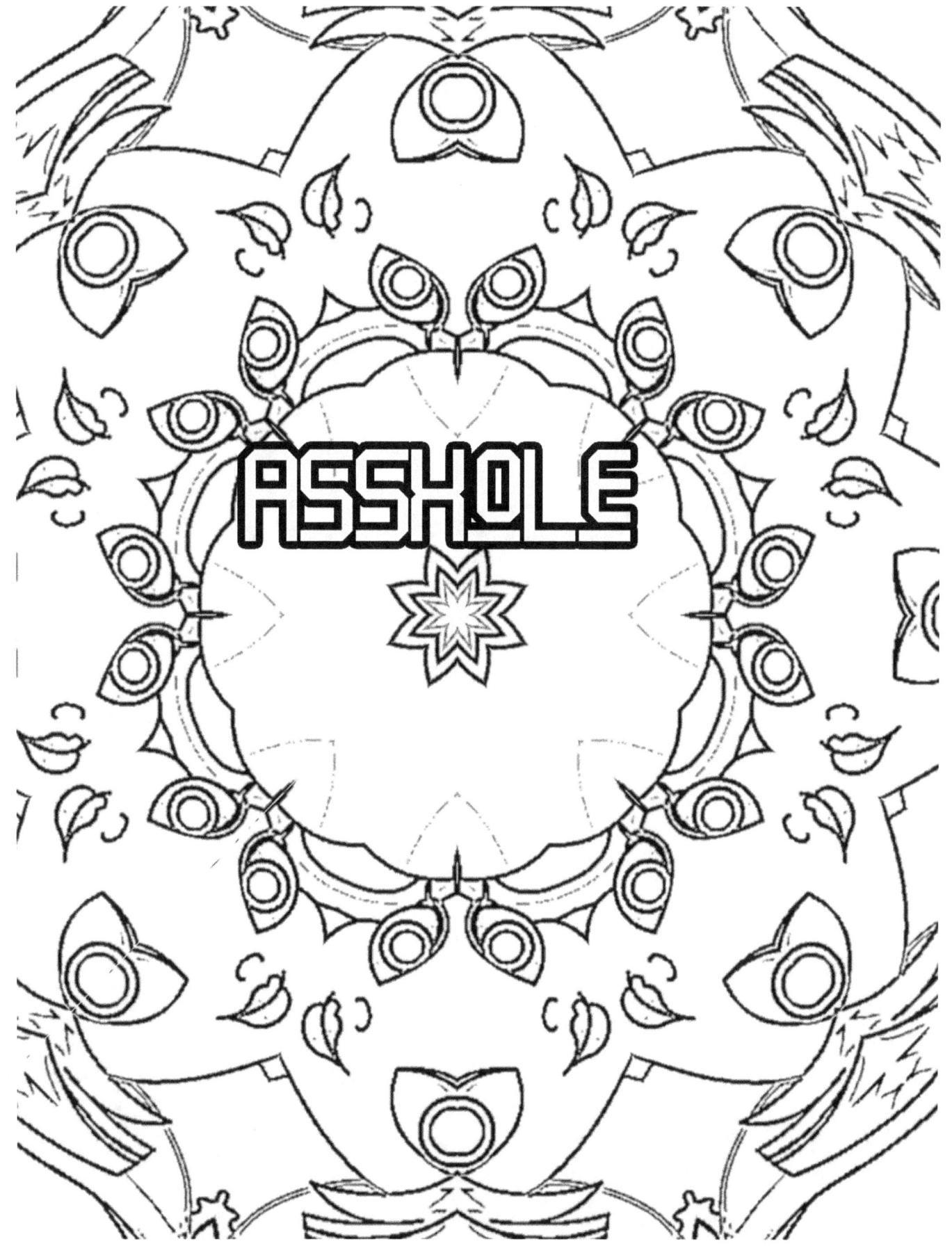

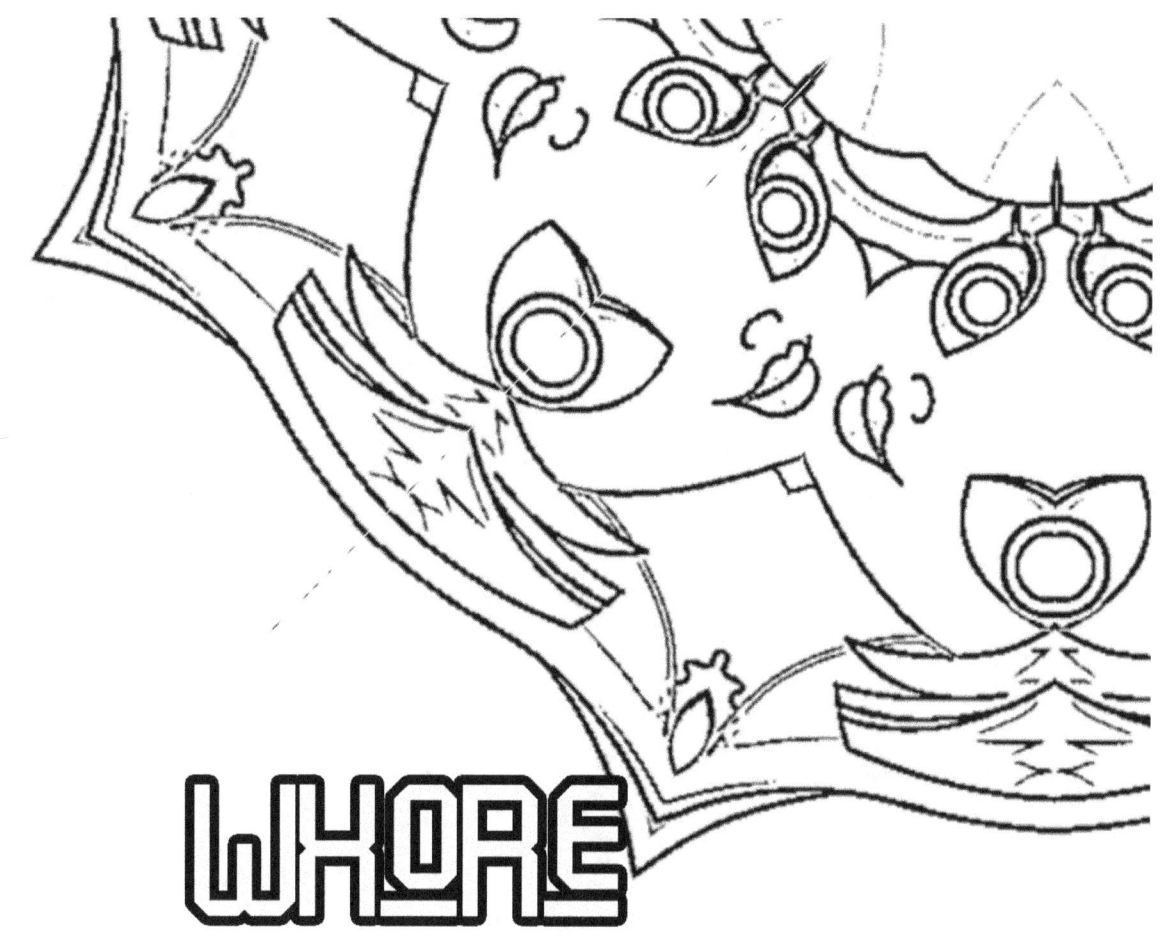

WHORE

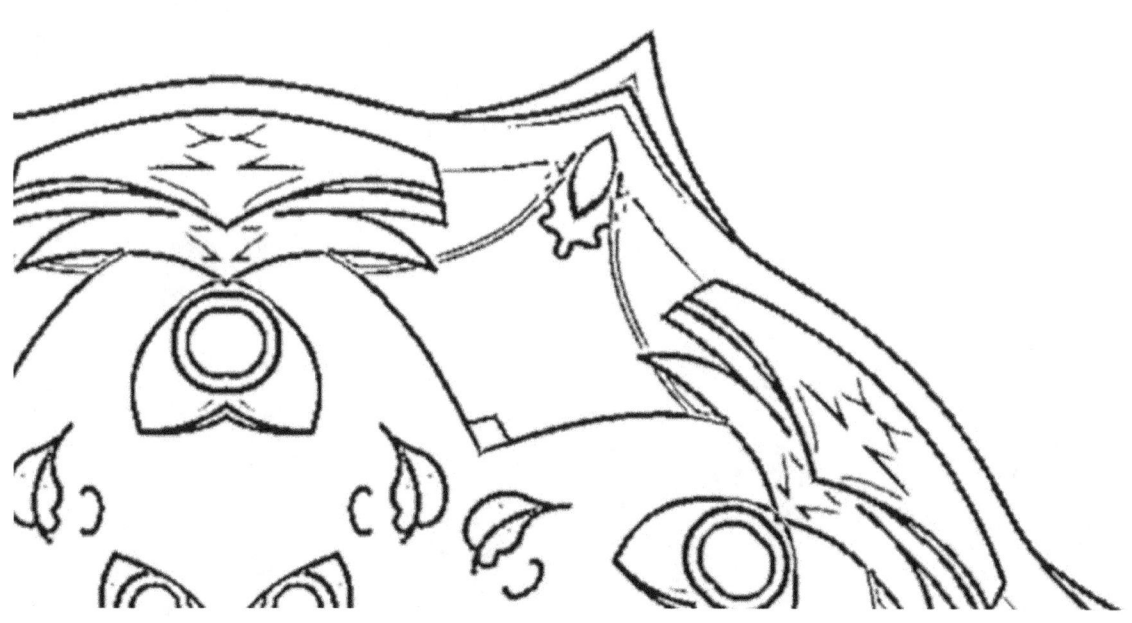

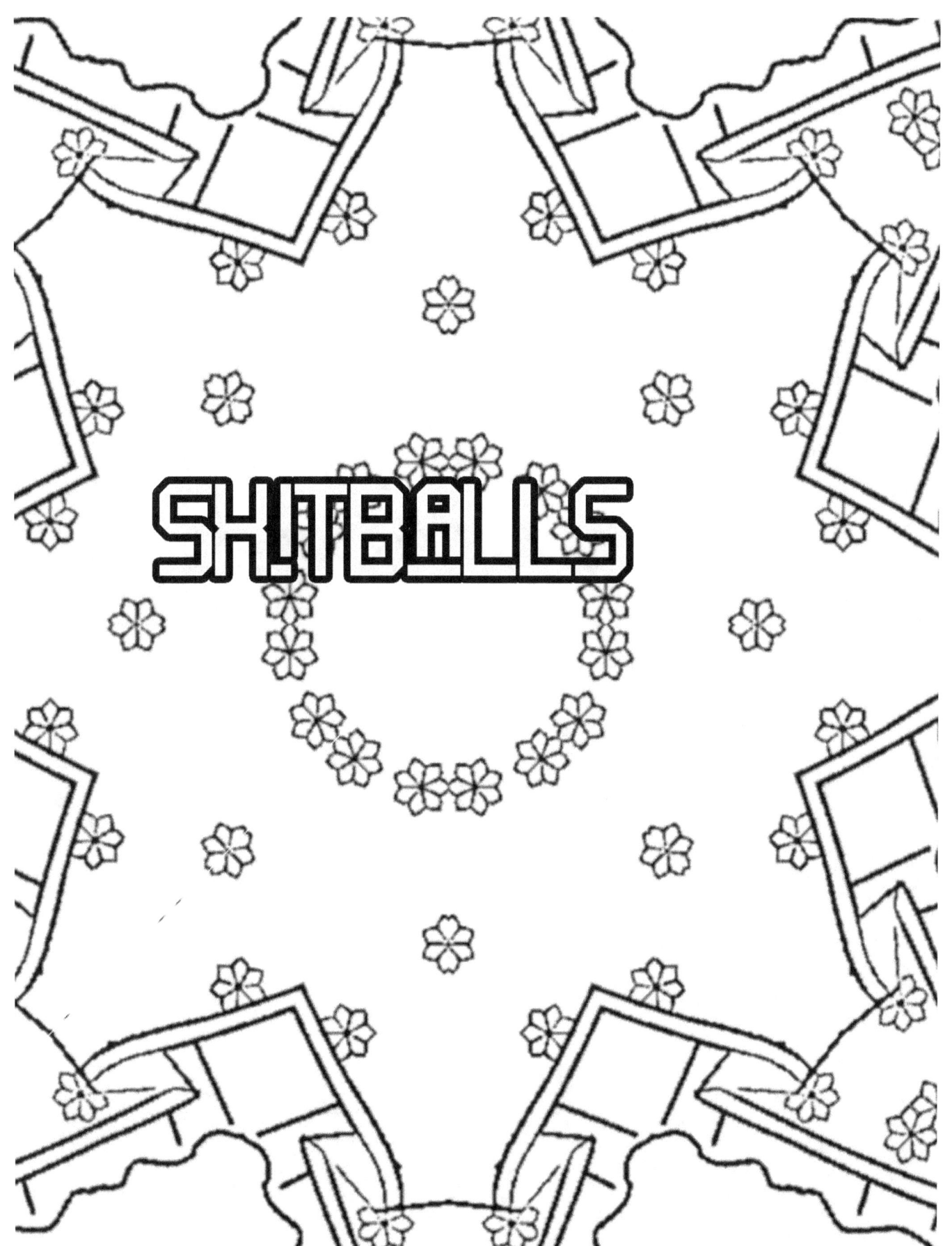

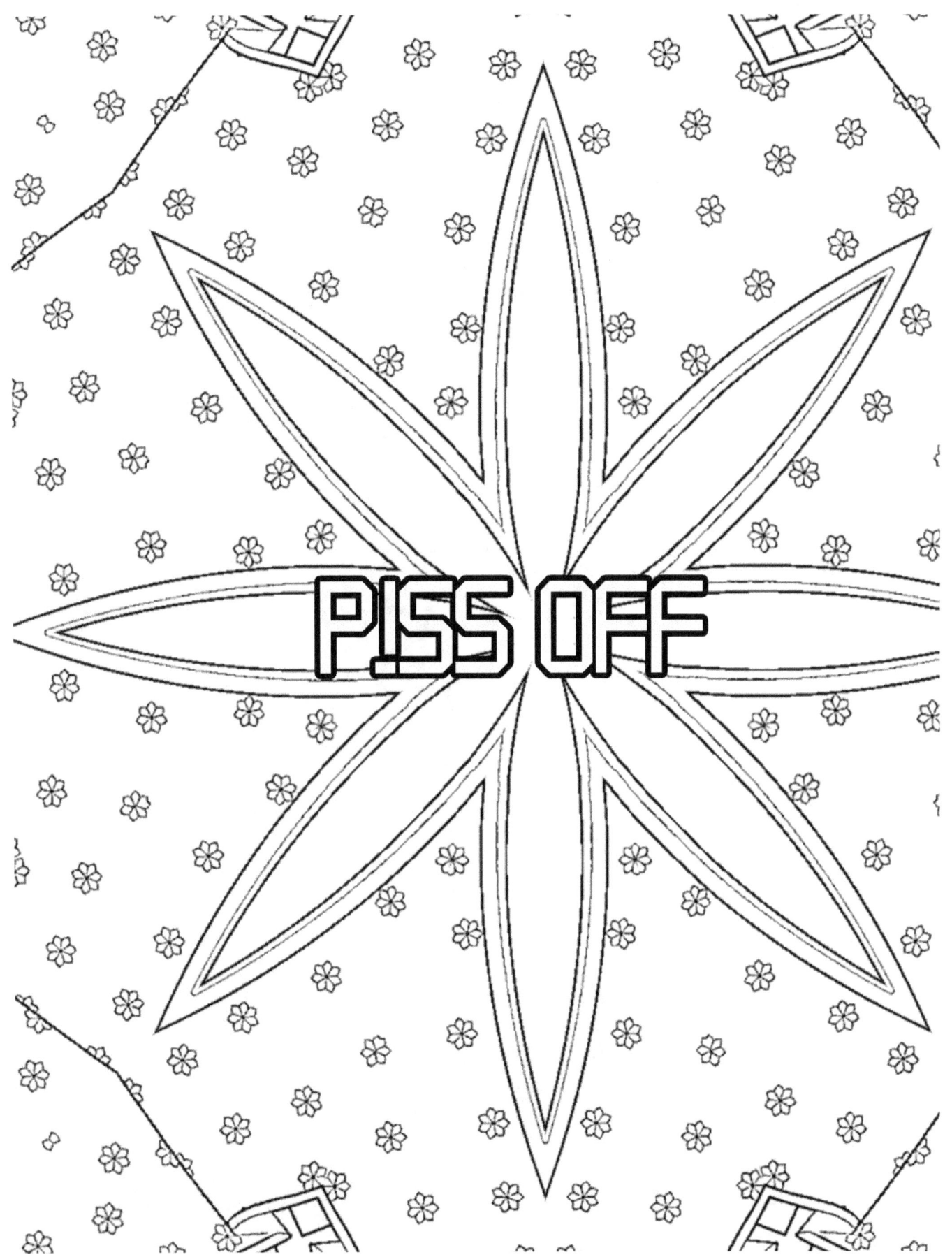

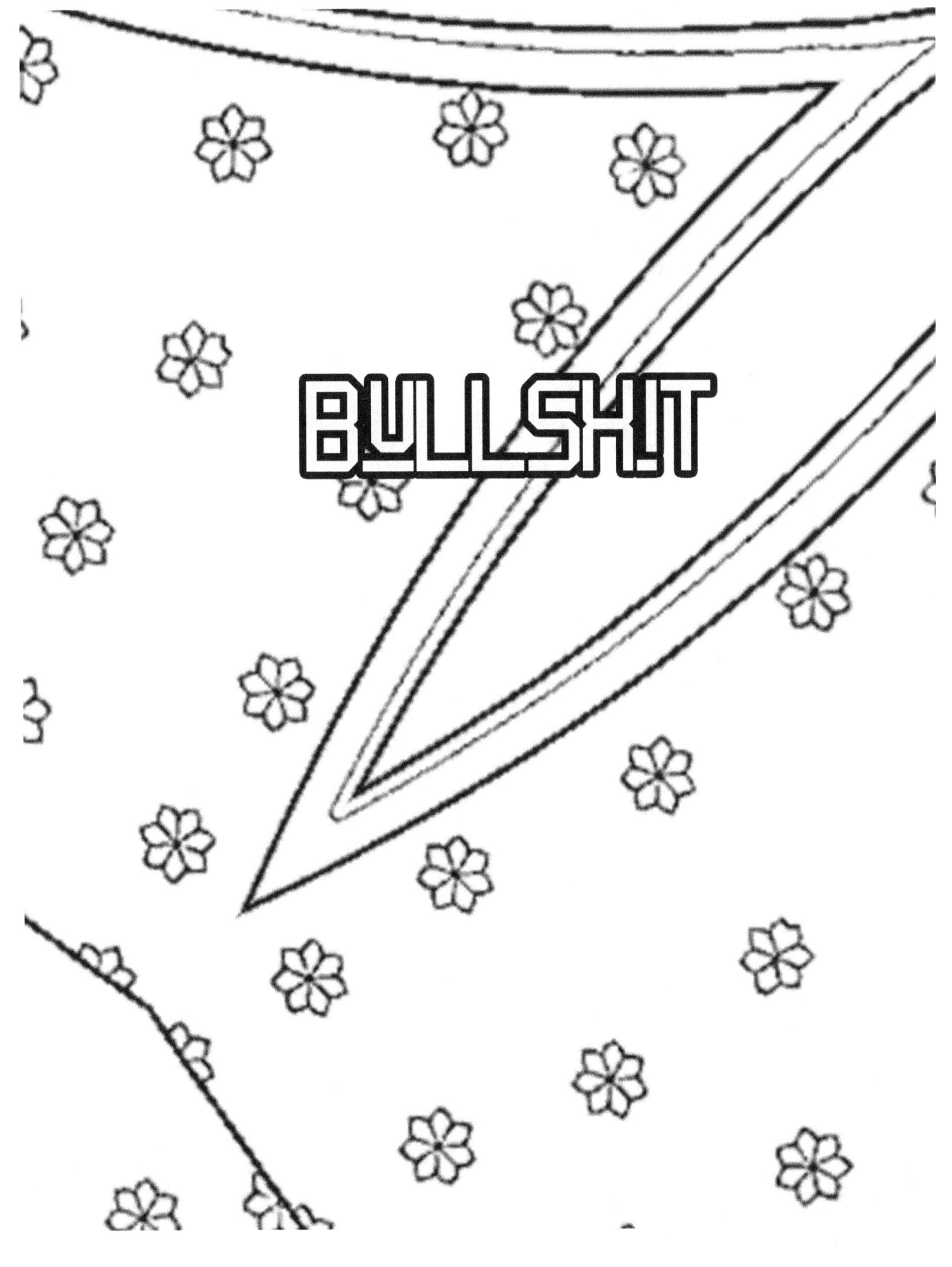

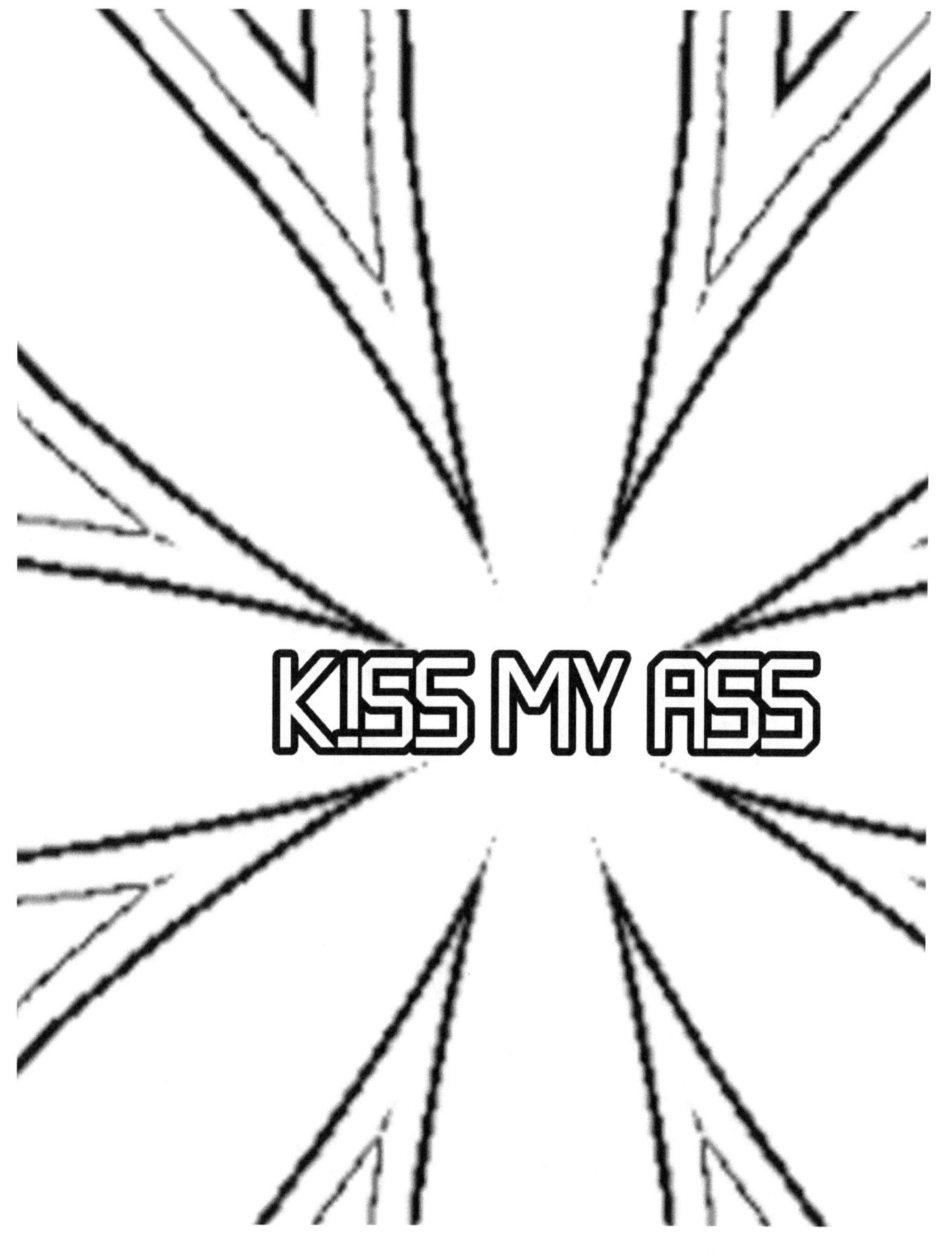

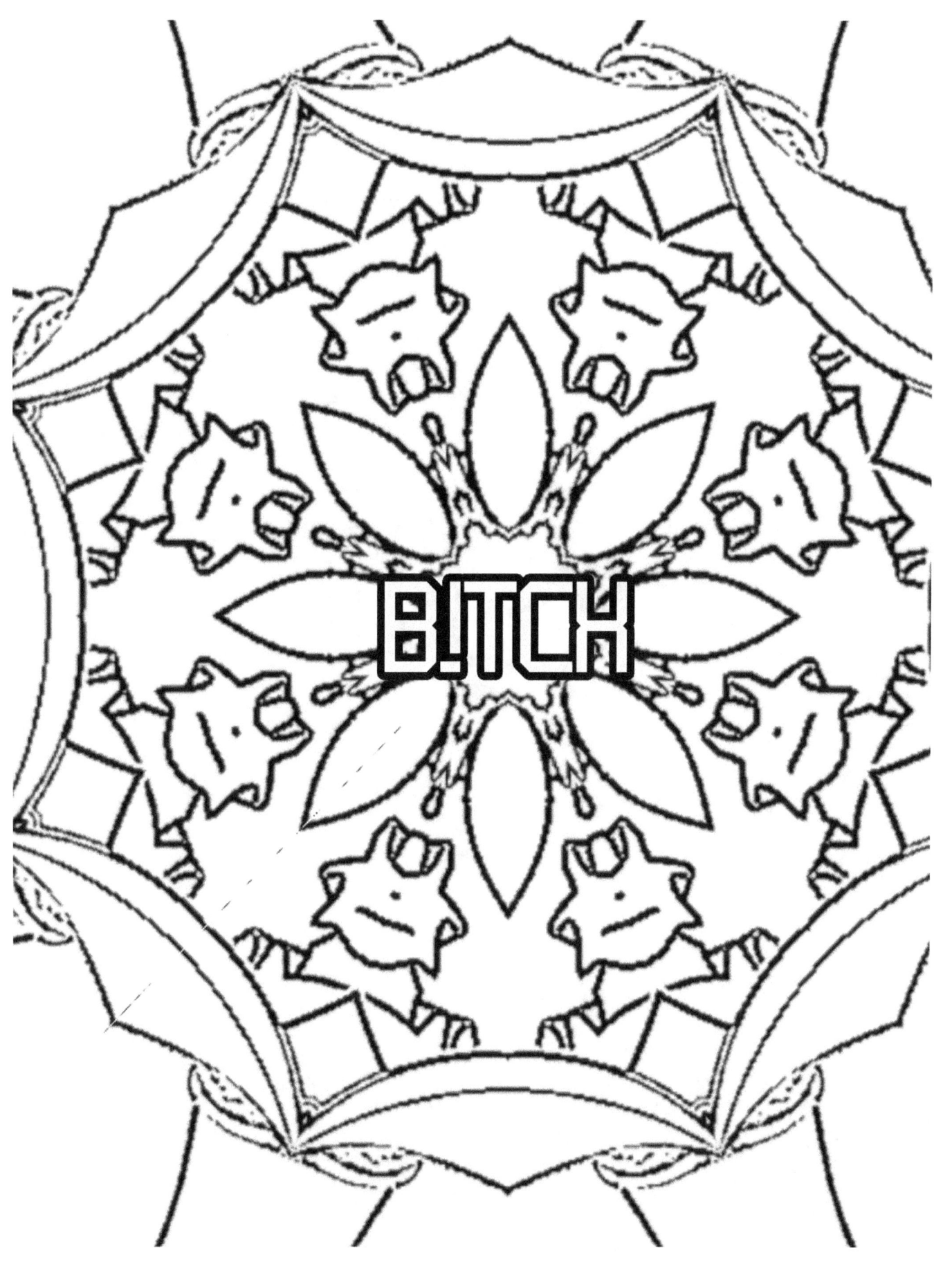

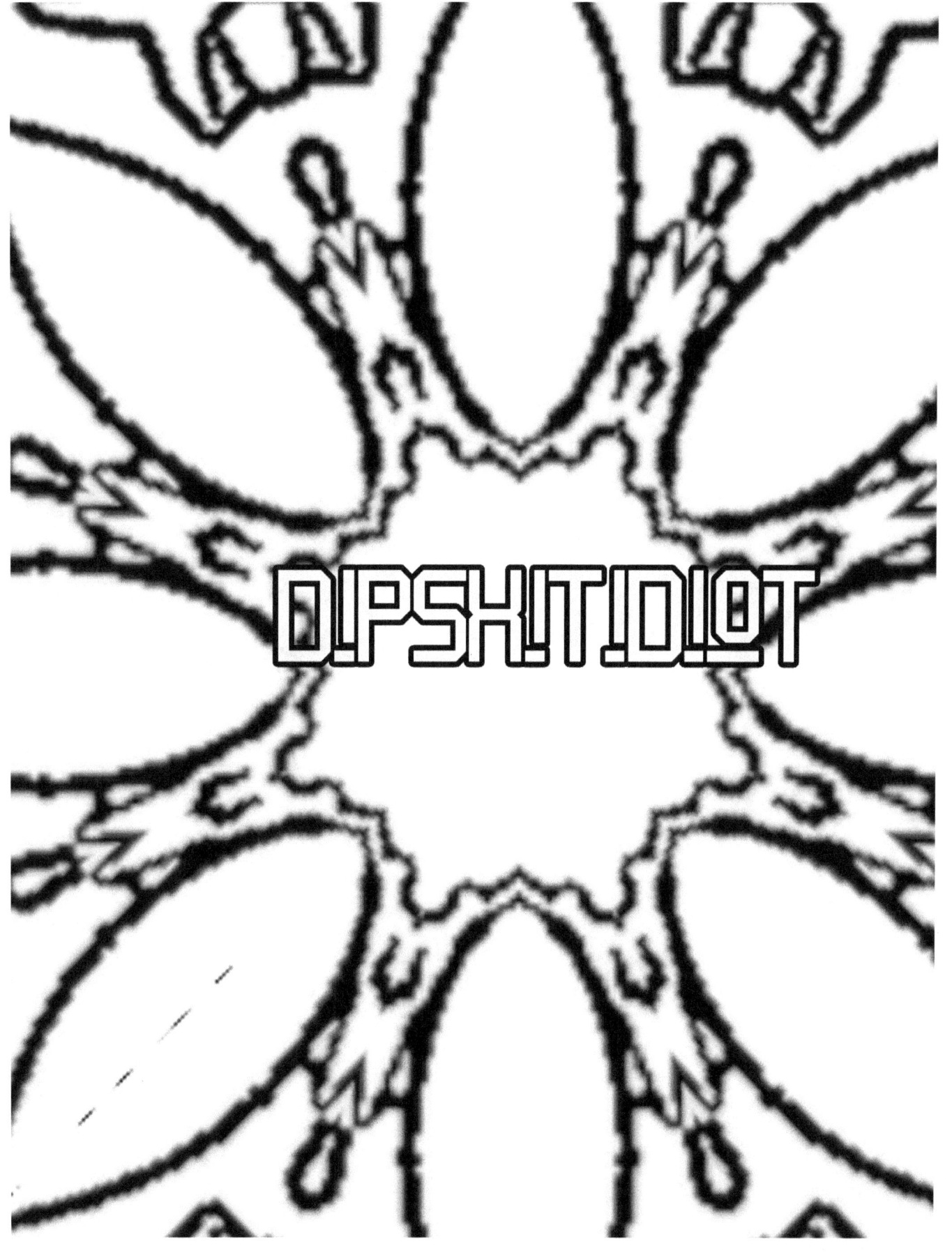

UGLY B!G SHOES

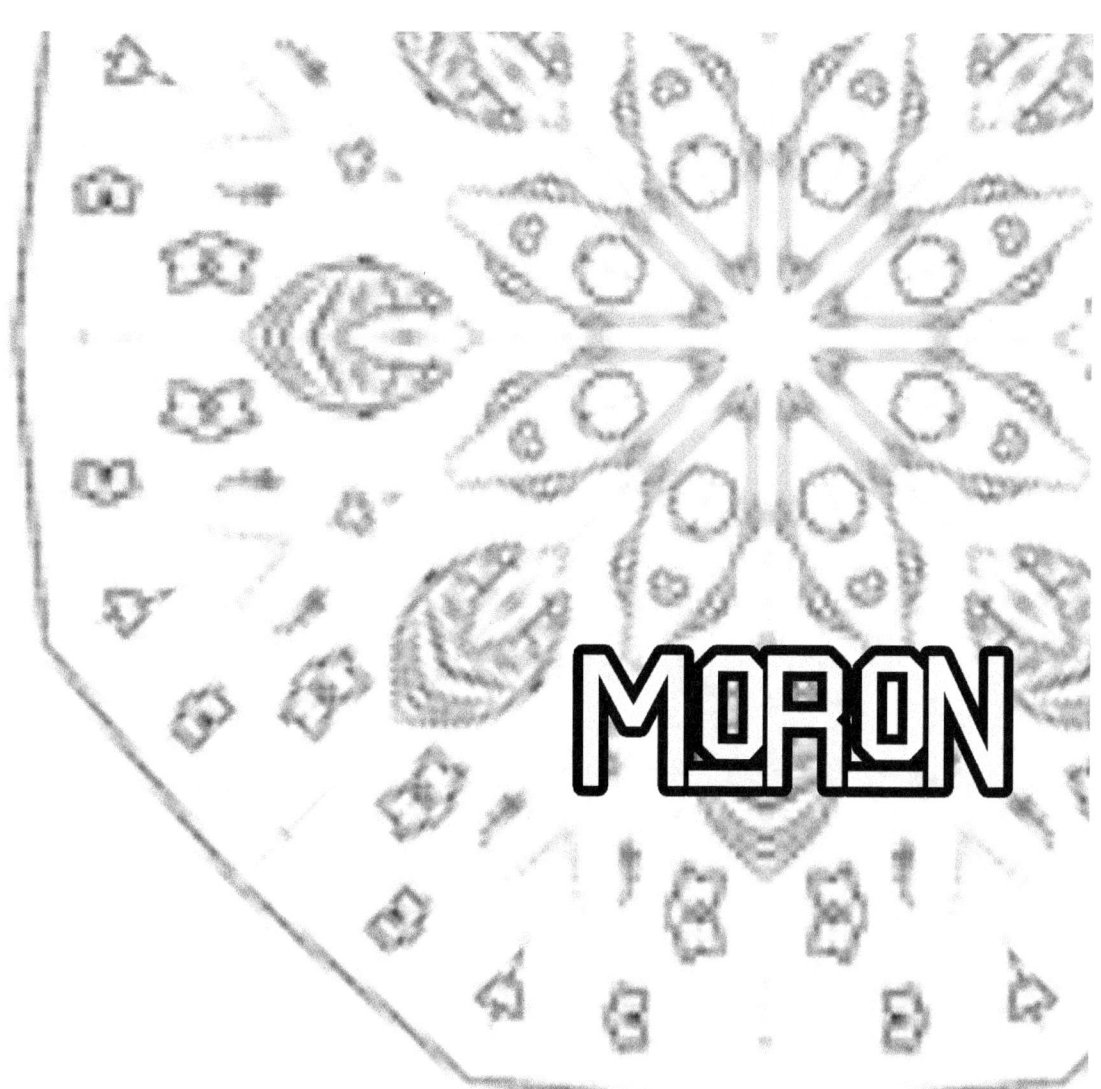

# FUCK A DUCK

# DOUCHE BAG

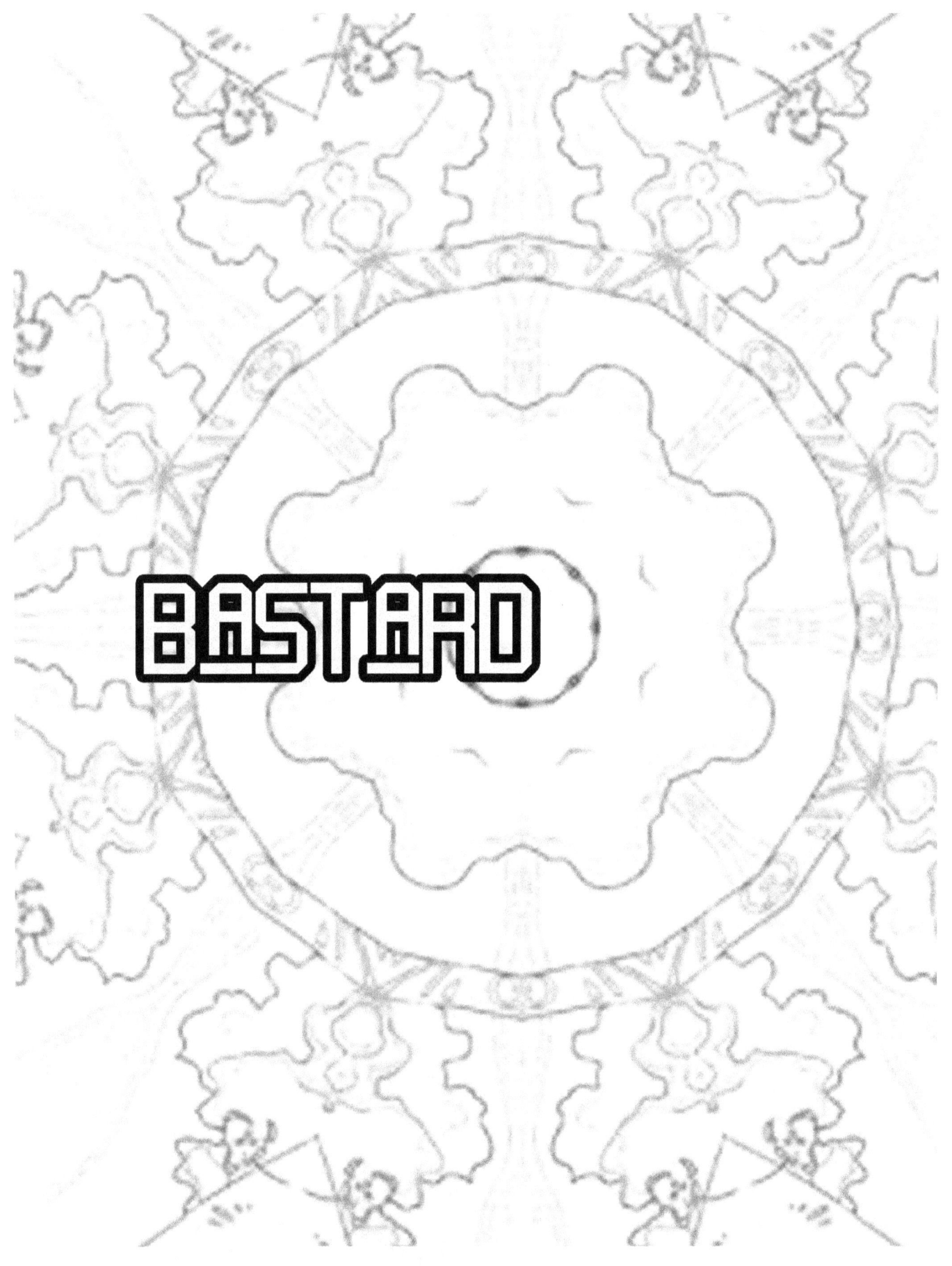

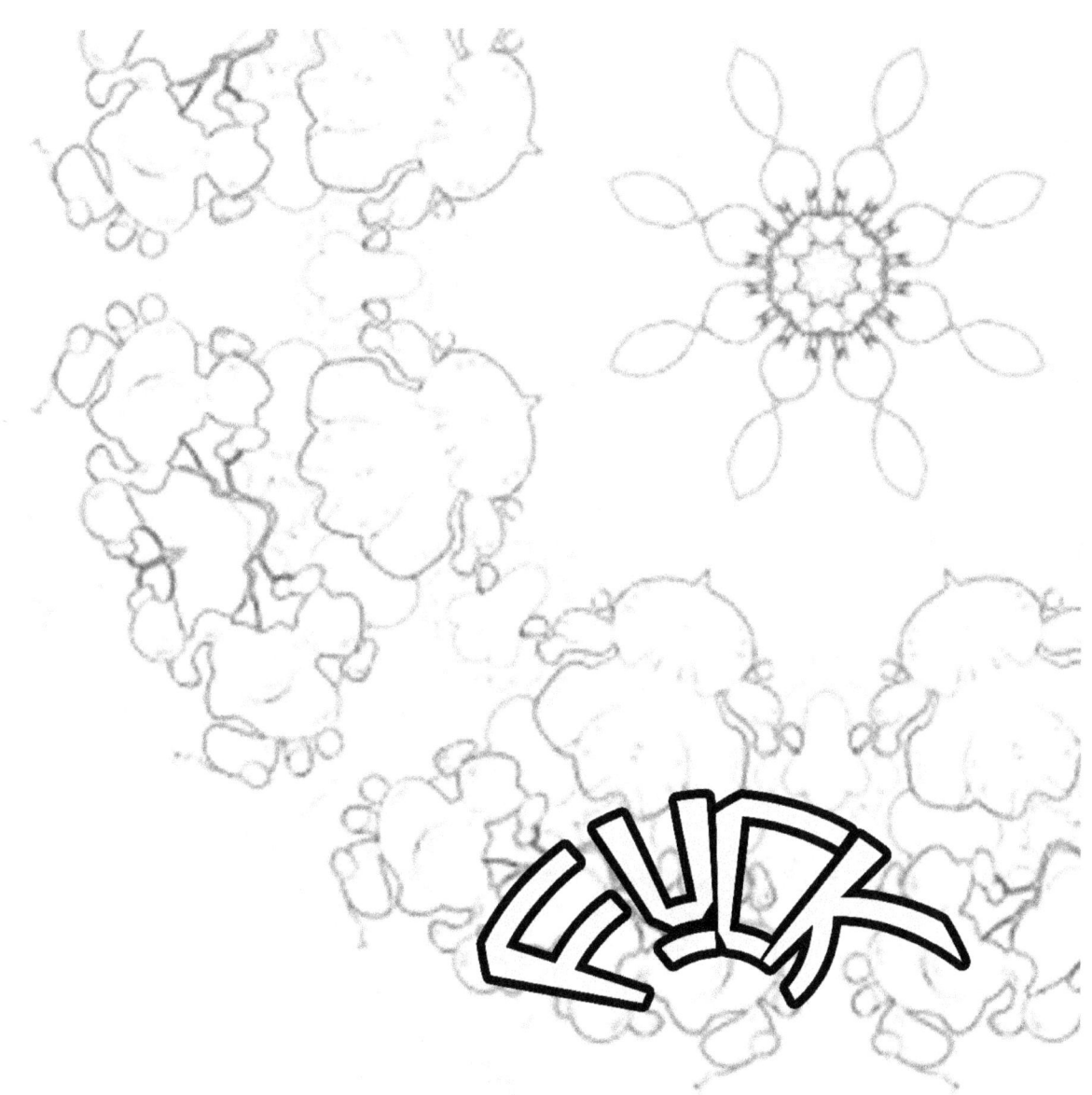

HOLY SH!T

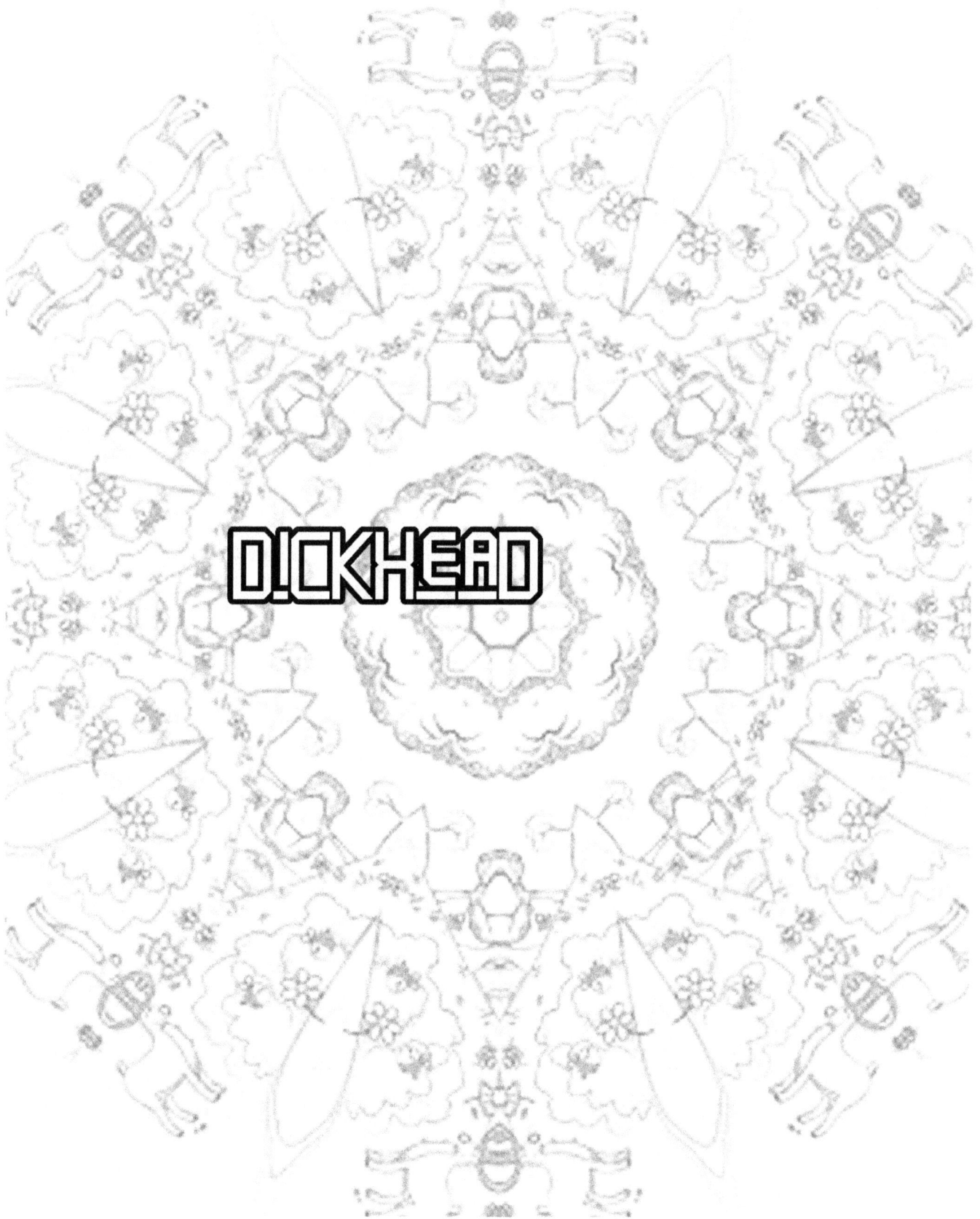

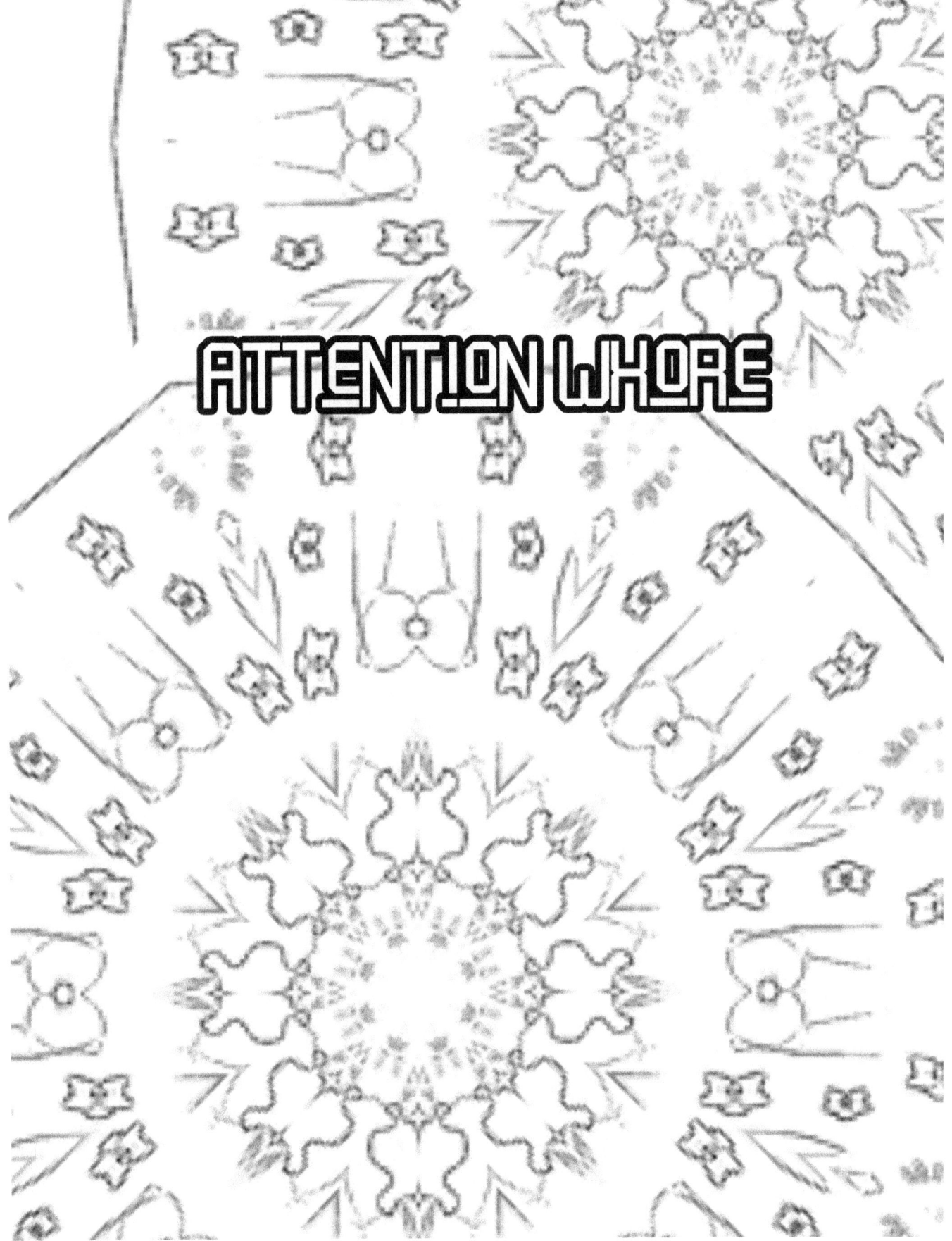

ATTENTION WHORE

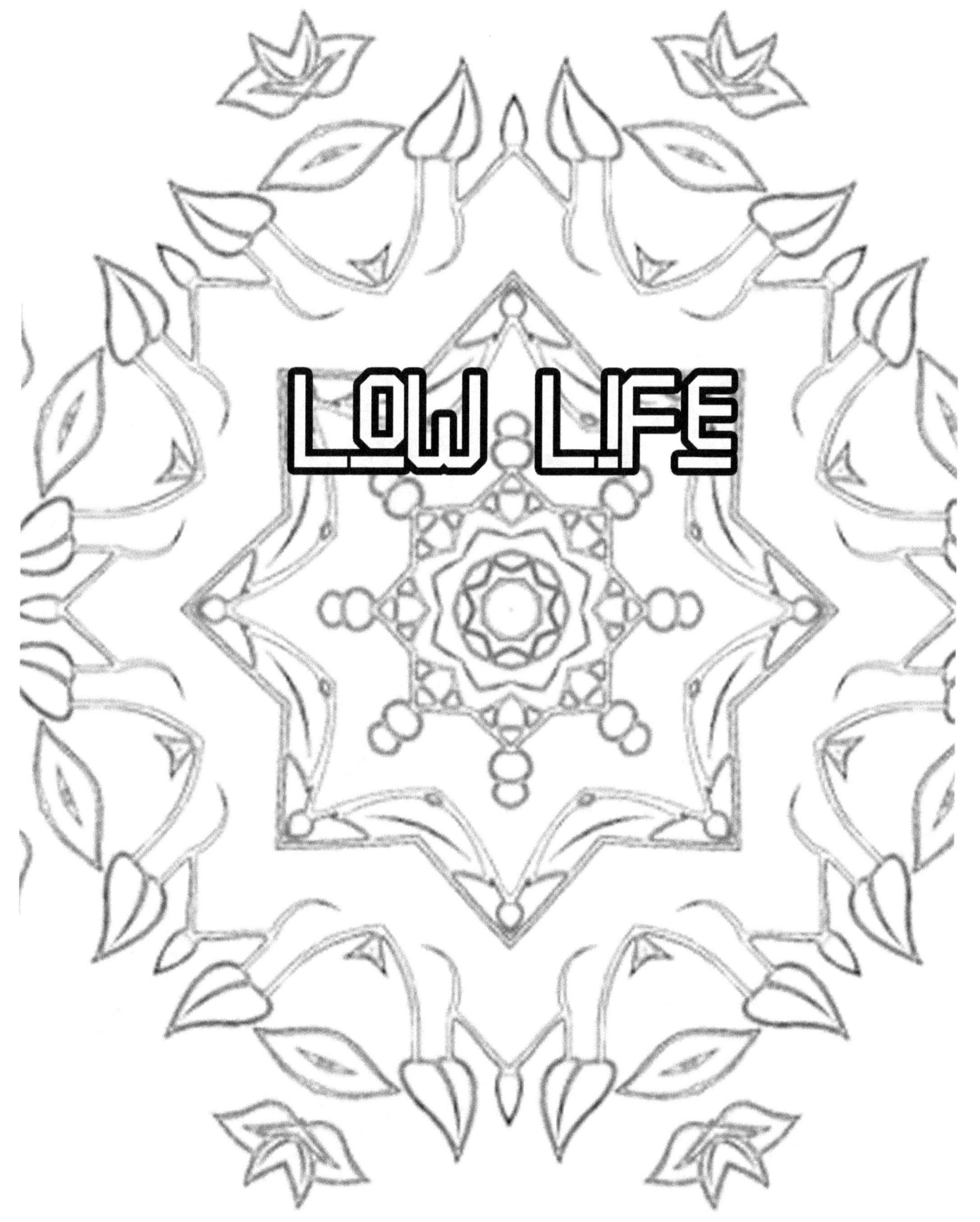

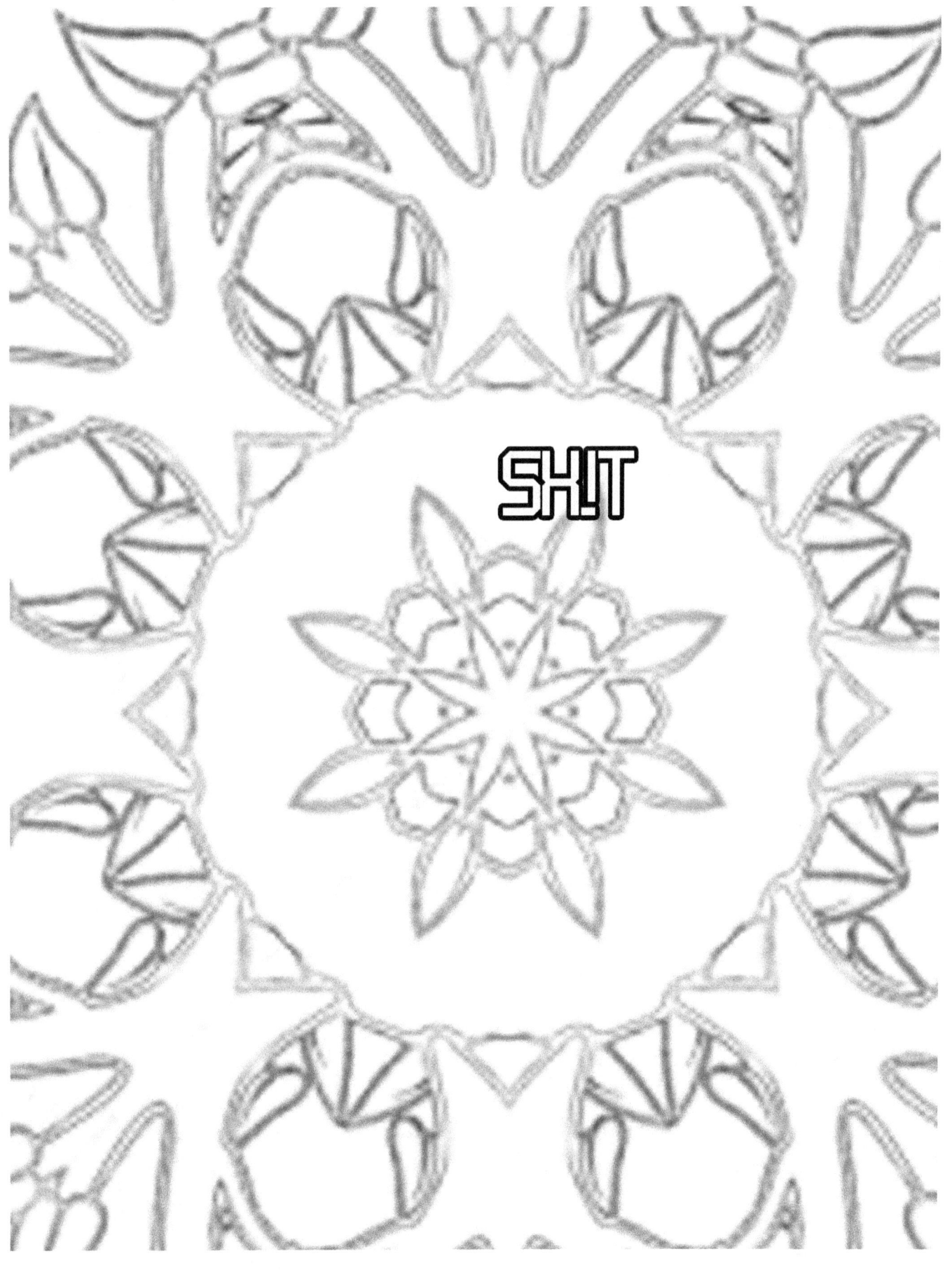

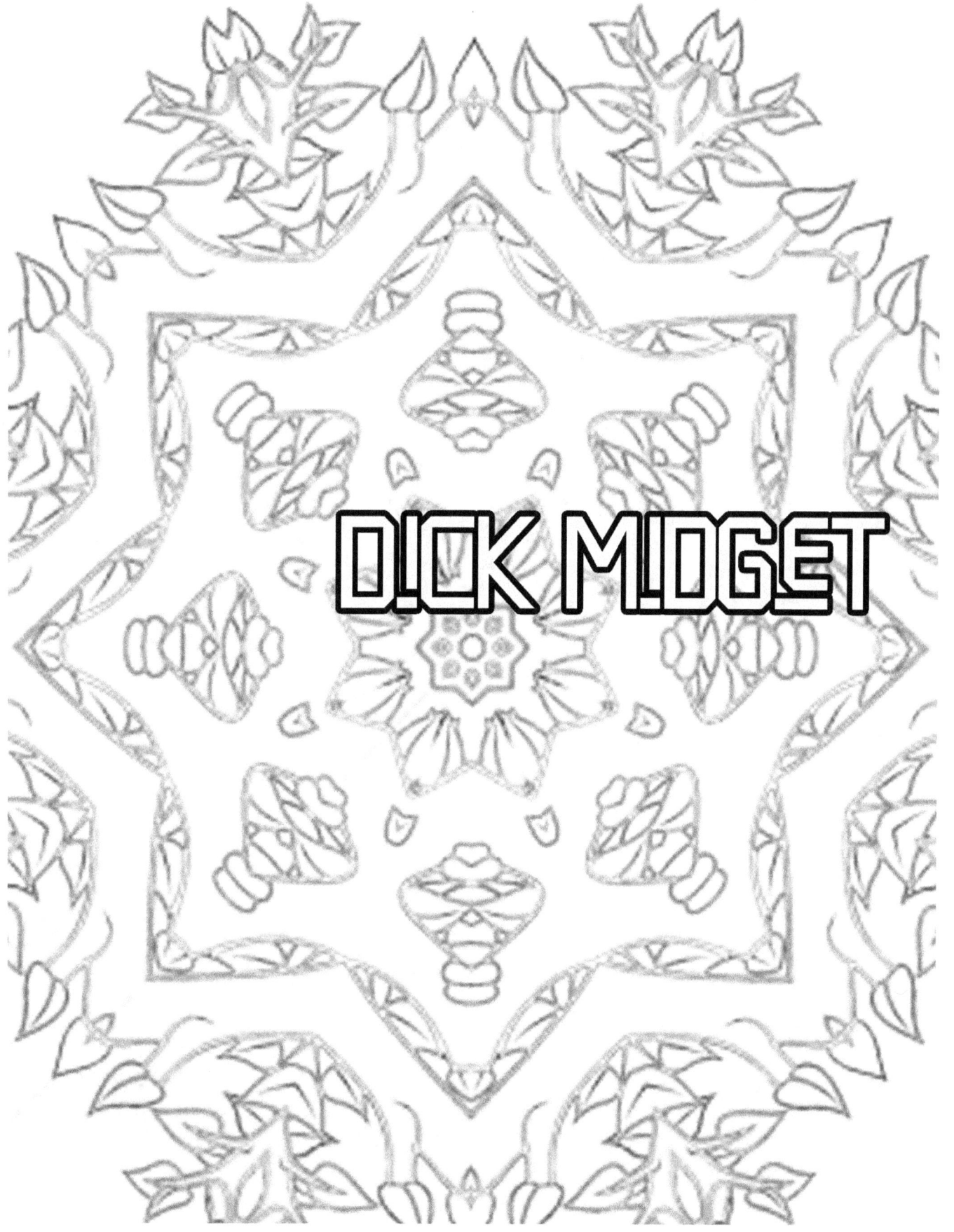